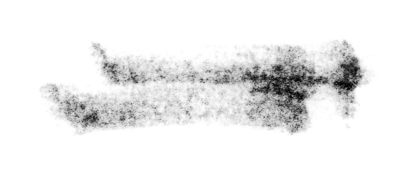

Salmon

Written by Deborah Hodge

Illustrated by Nancy Gray Ogle

KIDS CAN PRESS

WILDLIFE SERIES

Kids Can Press

For Alexandra, the newest member of our family, with love — DH
To my mother, Lois — NGO

For manuscript review and consultation, I am grateful to Dr. Robert Devlin, Head of the
Molecular Biology Program, Fisheries and Oceans Canada, Vancouver, BC; Dr. Richard Beamish,
Senior Scientist, Pacific Biological Station, Nanaimo, BC; Kim Fulton (Dr. Fish), Vice Principal,
Armstrong Elementary School, Armstrong, BC; Peter G. Amiro, Atlantic Salmon Biologist,
Bedford Institute of Oceanography, Fisheries and Oceans Canada, Halifax, NS; Esther Amiro, Librarian,
John W. MacLeod Elementary School, Halifax, NS; and Art McKay, Atlantic Salmon Federation,
Bocabec, NB. Thanks also to Dr. Robert Devlin; Drew Devlin, Teacher, Parkcrest Elementary School;
and Jennifer Stone, Technical Artist, all of Vancouver, BC, for reviewing the illustrations.

For expert editing, I thank Lori Burwash and Valerie Wyatt. Thank you also to
Marie Bartholomew, Series Designer; Valerie Hussey, Publisher; Rivka Cranley, Editor-in-Chief;
Brigitte Shapiro, Sales and Marketing Director; Fred Horler, U.S. Marketing Manager;
and Joan Yolleck, U.S. Sales Manager. It's a pleasure to work with you all!

Kids Can Press acknowledges the financial support of
the Ontario Arts Council, the Canada Council for the
Arts and the Government of Canada, through the BPIDP,
for our publishing activity.

Published in Canada by
Kids Can Press Ltd.
29 Birch Avenue
Toronto, ON M4V 1E2

Published in the U.S. by
Kids Can Press Ltd.
2250 Military Road
Tonawanda, NY 14150

www.kidscanpress.com

Edited by Lori Burwash
Designed by Marie Bartholomew
Printed and bound in Hong Kong by Book Art Inc., Toronto

The hardcover edition of this book is smyth sewn
casebound.
The paperback edition of this book is limp sewn with
a drawn-on cover.

CM 02 0 9 8 7 6 5 4 3 2 1
CM PA 02 0 9 8 7 6 5 4 3 2 1

**National Library of Canada Cataloguing in
Publication Data**

Hodge, Deborah
    Salmon

(Kids Can Press wildlife series)
Includes index.

ISBN 1-55074-961-7 (bound)
ISBN 1-55074-963-3 (pbk.)

1. Salmon — Juvenile literature. I. Ogle, Nancy Gray.
II. Title. III. Series.

QL638.S2H63 2002   j597.5'6   C2001-901000-1

Kids Can Press is a Nelvana company

Contents

Salmon

Salmon are graceful swimmers. Their long silver bodies glide through the water.

Salmon are fish. Fish have gills for breathing and fins for swimming. Fish have backbones. Their bodies are covered with scales. Baby fish hatch from eggs.

These Atlantic salmon are swimming in the ocean.

SALMON FACT

Some salmon can leap up to 3 m (10 feet). This is higher than a soccer goalpost.

Salmon are strong. They can leap up waterfalls and swim against powerful currents. This is a coho salmon.

Kinds of salmon

There are two main kinds of salmon: Pacific salmon and Atlantic salmon. Some species of Pacific salmon are sockeye, chum, pink, coho, chinook, steelhead and masu. There is only one species of Atlantic salmon.

A salmon is silver for most of its life. It changes color when it is ready to spawn – produce eggs. The salmon on these pages are shown in both their silver and spawning colors. Their average weights are also given.

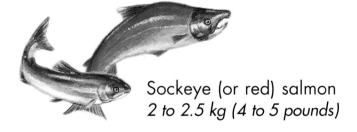

Pink (or humpback) salmon
1.5 to 2.5 kg (3 to 5 pounds)

Masu salmon
1 to 4.5 kg (2 to 10 pounds)

Sockeye (or red) salmon
2 to 2.5 kg (4 to 5 pounds)

Coho (or silver) salmon
2.5 to 5.5 kg (5 to 12 pounds)

Steelhead salmon
1.5 to 4 kg (3 to 9 pounds)

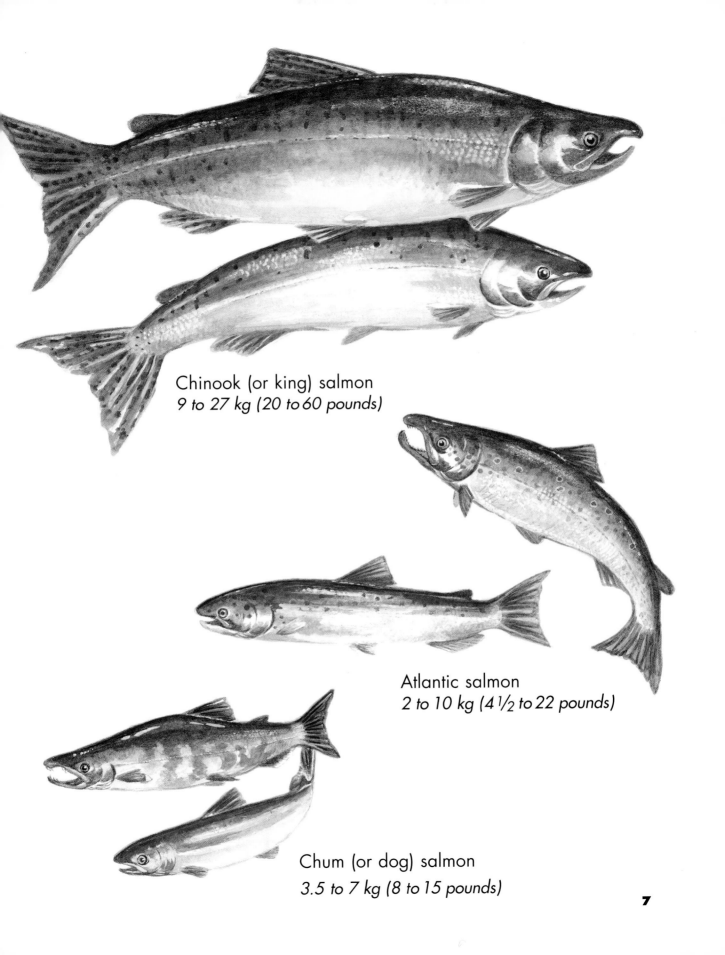

Chinook (or king) salmon
9 to 27 kg (20 to 60 pounds)

Atlantic salmon
2 to 10 kg (4 1/2 to 22 pounds)

Chum (or dog) salmon
3.5 to 7 kg (8 to 15 pounds)

Where salmon live

Salmon are born in freshwater streams. When they are old enough, they swim to the salty ocean. Here, they grow into adults. When salmon are ready to spawn, they swim back to the streams where they hatched – their home streams.

Wherever they live, salmon need clean, cool water. Cool water carries the oxygen that salmon breathe. Cool water also helps salmon eggs hatch at the right time. If the water is too warm, the eggs hatch early – before there is food in the stream for the baby salmon.

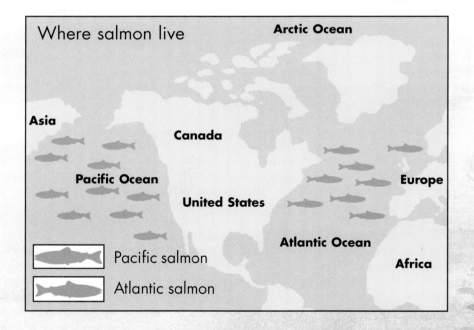

Where salmon live

Arctic Ocean

Asia

Canada

Pacific Ocean

United States

Europe

Atlantic Ocean

Africa

Pacific salmon

Atlantic salmon

Salmon live in northern areas, where the water is cool.

Salmon are one of the few fish that live in both freshwater and saltwater.

A salmon stream has gravel and running water. Trees shade the stream and keep it cool. Floating plants and insects are food for baby salmon.

Salmon bodies

A salmon's body is built for swimming. This is a pink salmon.

Skin

A salmon's color helps it hide. From above, its dark back blends in with shadows in the water. From below, its silver belly looks like light on the water's surface.

Scales

Scales on top of the skin protect the salmon. They are covered with a slime that helps the salmon glide through the water.

Gills

A salmon breathes with gills. Water goes in the mouth and out the gills. The gills soak up oxygen in the water and pass it through the body.

Lateral line

Tiny pores in a salmon's lateral line feel movement. They tell the salmon when food or enemies are near.

Fins

The salmon swings its tail fin to swim. It uses its side fins to stop, turn and back up. Other fins are used for balance.

Bones and muscles

A salmon's backbone flexes when swimming. Strong tail muscles make the salmon go fast.

Swim bladder

A salmon fills its swim bladder by gulping air. When the swim bladder is full, the salmon can float.

Salmon life cycle

Over its lifetime, a salmon changes and grows.
It passes through a series of stages called a life cycle.

The life cycle of a chum salmon is shown
here. All salmon go through these
stages. To follow the stages,
start reading at #1.

2. Alevin

Eggs hatch into baby
salmon, called alevin.

1. Eggs

Salmon begin
as eggs in a stream.

6. Spawners

At the stream, spawners
lay and fertilize eggs. After
spawning, most Pacific
salmon die. Steelhead and
Atla ntic salmon swim
back to the ocean.

3. Fry

When alevin are ready to swim, they are called fry. Fry look like tiny fish.

The Atlantic salmon has an extra stage in its life cycle: the parr. A parr is a stage between the fry and the smolt.

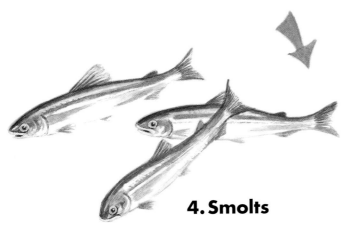

4. Smolts

When fry are silver and ready to swim to the ocean, they are called smolts.

5. Adults

In the ocean, smolts feed and grow into adults. When adult salmon are ready to spawn, they swim back to their home streams.

Baby salmon

A mother salmon lays her eggs in a stream – usually in the fall. She buries them in a hollow in the gravel, called a redd. The gravel helps hide the eggs from hungry birds, raccoons and other fish.

The eggs hatch in late winter or spring. A baby salmon, or alevin, is about as long as a pin. A yolk sac hangs from its middle. It provides the alevin with food. An alevin stays in the gravel until its yolk sac is gone – up to three months.

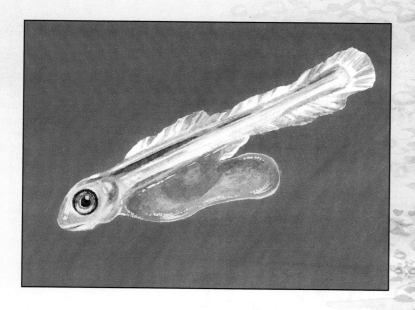

An alevin's yolk sac gets used up as the alevin grows. This is a close-up of a masu alevin.

Baby coho are growing inside these eggs. Their dark eyes show through. Some eggs have hatched. The alevin hide in the shadows.

Young salmon

Once its yolk sac is gone, a baby salmon is called a fry. A fry wriggles to the water's surface and gulps air. With its swim bladder full, this little fish can swim and hunt for food. Fry eat tiny plants and insects.

Chum and pink fry swim to the ocean soon after leaving the redd. Other species stay in lakes or streams for a year or more. When a young salmon is ready to go to the ocean, its skin turns silver. Now it is called a smolt.

As smolts swim to the ocean, they pass through an estuary — where a river meets an ocean. Here, they feed and get used to the ocean's salty water. These are sockeye smolts.

Stripes on a fry's body are called parr marks. The marks help these chinook fry hide.

This is a close-up of a salmon scale. Scientists know how old a salmon is by counting the rings on a scale. This scale shows that the salmon is five years old.

Adult salmon

Salmon become adults in the ocean. Here, the food is plentiful and there is space for them to grow. Salmon stay in the ocean for one to eight years, depending on the species.

In the ocean, salmon may swim thousands of kilometers (miles). They go to rich feeding areas in the north. They eat shrimp, squid and smaller fish, such as herring. Salmon also feed on plankton – tiny floating plants and animals.

Salmon travel in groups. This is safer than swimming alone. A seal is hunting these Atlantic salmon.

Chinook and Atlantic salmon spend the most time feeding in the ocean. This is why they are the biggest species.

This is a close-up of the tiny krill that some salmon eat. The krill's pink color makes a salmon's flesh turn red.

Migrating salmon

Salmon leave the ocean when they are ready to spawn – produce eggs. They swim back to their home streams. This is called migrating. A salmon uses its keen sense of smell to find its home stream. It follows the scent of the soil, plants and insects in the stream.

Migrating salmon swim up rivers. Hundreds travel in a group called a salmon run. The salmon battle the strong current. They leap over rocks and logs and up waterfalls. The journey is long and hard, but the salmon don't give up.

A migrating salmon does not eat. It lives off the fat and protein stored in its body.

Salmon – such as these chinook – may migrate as far as 3300 km (2000 miles) to their home streams. Along the way, some are eaten by grizzly bears or other enemies.

Spawning salmon

At the stream, it is time to spawn. The salmon's body has changed. Its skin may be red, green, purple or black. The male has a hooked jaw and long teeth. Some males have a hump on their back. These changes help a salmon find a mate of its own species.

The mother salmon fans her tail to scoop out a redd – a hollow in the stream's gravel. Within the redd, she digs several nests. She lays up to 1000 eggs in each. Then she covers them with gravel.

These sockeye salmon are spawning. As the mother lays the eggs, the father fertilizes them with white milt. Now the eggs can grow into baby salmon.

Male salmon battle with their sharp teeth. The strongest male will spawn with the female of his choice. These are chum salmon.

This Atlantic salmon is digging a nest.

A new life cycle begins

After spawning, the salmon are worn out. Their bodies are tired from the long journey.

The parents guard their eggs for a few days. Then, most Pacific salmon die. But steelhead and Atlantic salmon return to the ocean. They will spawn again in other years.

Under the gravel, the eggs are growing. New salmon will hatch in a few months.

The bodies of the salmon break down. They add nutrients to the stream that help new plants grow. These plants will be food for the baby salmon that hatch next season.

A strong Atlantic salmon may spawn up to seven times.

As one life cycle ends, another begins.

Salmon in the food chain

In nature, animals eat and are eaten. One creature is food for another. This is called a food chain. Salmon are part of the food chain.

Trout, otters, eels, raccoons and mergansers (fish-eating ducks) feed on salmon eggs and baby salmon. Ospreys, loons and herons like to eat smolts. In the ocean, tuna, cod, seals, sharks and whales feed on salmon.

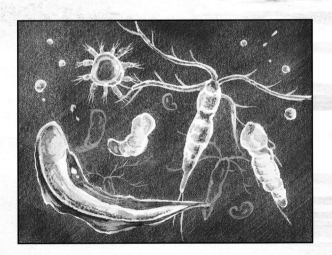

This is a close up of ocean plankton — an important part of the food chain. Salmon grow big feeding on plankton.

A salmon faces many dangers. Of 2500 eggs laid, only a few will become spawning adults.

Eagles, bears and other animals go to spawning rivers in the fall. They feed on dead and dying salmon. The animals depend on this rich food to stay alive.

Salmon and people

Salmon has always been an important food for North American people. But over time, too many fish were caught. The numbers of salmon kept dropping. Now there are strict rules about how many salmon can be fished.

To survive, salmon need food and clean, cool water. If harmful chemicals spill into the water, the salmon's food may be spoiled. When trees are cut from riverbanks, streams get too warm. The salmon get sick or their eggs hatch too soon.

Salmon depend on clean water and space to swim and grow. These sockeye salmon are migrating to their home stream.

Scientists count the salmon that return to spawn. This helps them decide how many can be fished.

Some salmon are born in a hatchery. Here, the babies are fed and protected until they are big enough to go to the ocean.

29

More salmon facts

Like all fish, a salmon has no eyelids. It sleeps with its eyes open.

The chinook salmon can weigh up to 55 kg (120 pounds) – as much as a large dog.

There are more pink salmon than any other kind of salmon.

The masu salmon lives only in Asia.

The chum salmon is found in more parts of the Pacific Ocean than any other salmon.

At spawning time, female salmon battle for the best sites to lay their eggs.

Salmon use the light of the sun and moon to find their way in the ocean.

The fish shown across these two pages is the smallest type of salmon. Look at the salmon on pages 6 and 7. Can you figure out which type it is?

It is a life-sized pink salmon. Other types of salmon are too big to fit on these pages.

Words to know

current: water in a river or ocean that flows strongly in one direction

estuary: the place where a river meets an ocean

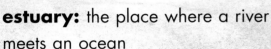

food chain: the series of one species eating another and then being eaten itself, and so on

home stream: the stream where a salmon hatches and spawns

life cycle: the series of stages a salmon passes through in its lifetime

mate: a male or female partner in a pair of salmon

migrate: to travel from one home to another, often as the seasons change

redd: a hollow in the gravel of a stream bed where a salmon lays her eggs

spawn: to produce salmon eggs. A mother salmon lays the eggs and the father fertilizes them.

Index